HELEN OR MY HUNGER

GALE MARIE
THOMPSON

HELEN OR MY HUNGER

YESYES BOOKS
Portland

COVER ART: "PINNED GHOST" © EMILIO VILLALBA

COVER & INTERIOR DESIGN: ALBAN FISCHER

ISBN 978-1-936919-84-0

PRINTED IN THE UNITED STATES OF AMERICA

LIBRARY OF CONGRESS CATALOGING-IN-PUBLICATION

DATA IS AVAILABLE UPON REQUEST.

PUBLISHED BY YESYES BOOKS

1614 NE ALBERTA ST

PORTLAND, OR 97211

YESYESBOOKS.COM

KMA SULLIVAN, PUBLISHER

STEVIE EDWARDS, SENIOR EDITOR, BOOK DEVELOPMENT

ALBAN FISCHER, GRAPHIC DESIGNER

COLE HILDEBRAND, SENIOR EDITOR OF OPERATIONS

AMBER RAMBHAROSE, EDITOR, INSTAGRAM

ALEXIS SMITHERS, ASSISTANT EDITOR, VINYL & YYB FACEBOOK

PHILLIP B. WILLIAMS, COEDITOR IN CHIEF, *VINYL*

AMIE ZIMMERMAN, EVENTS COORDINATOR

For Caroline Cabrera and Anne Cecelia Holmes,
mis medias naranjas

"Helen—Helen—Helen—
there was always another and another and another"

—H.D., *Helen in Egypt*

"—so I found
That Hunger—was a way
Of Persons outside Windows,
The Entering—takes away."

—EMILY DICKINSON

CONTENTS

HELEN OR MY HUNGER

I wait to come to good. I wait carved
from the same war, draped by the mechanism
between myself and fabric pleasure,
how pressed, how shut. The icon I remember
is ragged and full of brown cardinals.
It sees me, parallel shoulders and not.
The young thing in a frame.
A slow press of film I wait for to ripen.

I am asking this of you. To see things out of order.
My body's floor bright and fixed with you,
clay mask powder in the tub and sink.
The finest way to avoid is through the body,
getting out so quickly it doesn't deserve
the name of leaving. I reveal the ship's bone
like a stammer. I magnet a napkin of sage
to the fridge, fruit fly blood on my fingers.

To name her is desire. To name her is a violence.

Helen is no Helen, but is she lack or artifact? A gash of solidness, a wooden bowl of teeth to break the narrative. A mother whose fingers tic against your wrist, one by one. The mark carries over and over.

But she is a beautiful body to mark, this body as speech act. A beautiful body that swells slowly, expands, empties. Naturally, too, she is nude, a mass of protein in blue ink. Her nude body, filled with charcoal. Teeth of charcoal. You can palpate the gold, peeling crust of her. You can palpate her.

To long for a subject is a lack, must be desire. But it is a retreat further into the cage.

I bite her image close to the knuckle. I call her *wine-dark* in her cloister, her gathered rotundities.

I didn't want to find Helen.

I never find Helen.

I want to write to the *Eidolon*.

I want a place/person/name toward whom to address the breach.

With lemon voices they called you *hated Helen*.
They called you *Eidolon, Eikon*.

In the cooked tin sheet I can see her face—yours—
eyes scooped out and over. Sands shift, pull down
into a strip. You are no one's mother.

I have placed all of this in you, Helen. I am
scratching it out, groove-voiced. This is not an embrace
but a crimp, a coil. I breathe out to talk to you,
am suddenly not my own.

If I am a creature with a sense of time—of passage, lapse, rupture
or ekstasis—I can be said to remember.

I foam trees at the mouth and approach story.

I'm thinking of nonsense now, Helen: June a gash of poplar, and the silver light on my chest at four in the morning. Rereading a big astronomy book on the counter at the hotel restaurant where I work. *Married with Children* on the television above the bar.

I eat two mini croissants and a pistachio muffin and vomit sugar in the bathroom stall. I eat pineapple and keep it down.

Perhaps I would like to have more than one body, this one too dismantled. Too carnivorous. Mistaking morning for salvage. *Helen, you are right to worry*, I want to say. I have nothing to give and it tastes sour. Sometimes in this story I cannot read the traces, or half-turn my head but for some dim mirror.

I dress in the dark, and no one knows.

Mermaid, myth, bloom of breast and carpenter: always, Helen, you drown, lose your shiny peel of memory, mark frame and frame by incision. You drown and I carve slabs of wax. You fast before men who will have you in this house, men peering over their glasses of beautiful, beautiful.

I write from the belly of the *I*, the breaking of the fan. I read and need it to fold me. The only name for this is *palimpsest*, to go over the tangle again and again.

In dreams I carry women on my back.

It was the wet bridge of rupture.

It was when I was seven, playing in the snow, and I accidentally split my lavender corduroys at the crotch. I felt it in my throat, I felt it sore and bile-sick. I wanted to keep my fingers in the tear, to swallow down my own dark recording.

A year or so later I was caught watching TV and cutting tiny holes into my favorite green smocked dress with left-handed craft scissors. Nothing cleared the pit, but nothing gave me a deeper pleasure: the hum of my stomach, my legs in their crossed position, cupping me, keeping me inside. A feeling associated with later, deeper cuts.

Is it better to leave the ruins behind, to leave the old language, or to sit inside it, the economy of gapes? And how can I offer these gapes to you?

Where the scar gathers itself, the upward itch of pain.

Violence is what brought H.D. back to Helen, each decade a new layer of war. The endless loop of ruin—of, as she writes in her notes, a *Holocauste*.

Like Stesichorus, like Euripedes, H.D. removes Helen from Troy. Like Stesichorus, like Euripedes, H.D. places her in Egypt and sends an *eidolon*, a double, in her place to be fought over. According to the *Pallinode* of Stesichorus, H.D. writes, *Helen was never in Troy. She had been transposed or translated from Greece into Egypt, leaving the substitute in her place. The Greeks and the Trojans alike fought for an illusion.*[1]

Eidolon, an ancient Greek word meaning: a representation of the form of an object; a phantom, or look-alike of the human form.

The echo of an echo.

Helen's first function is to be the sign.

I wake to the quiet points of my instrument.
A weighty topography to posture. Mewling myth
of sandals, full-stepped
into sand, the silver gelatin
of growing-up. A posture, and yet
elsewhere footage of the reenactment,
elsewhere my pierce, bone alarmingly definite.

The poem disappears, Helen.
The poem says nothing
unless it comes back answered.
Like a myth, it bleeds at the edges.
Where to stop and start is a postcard hung by a pin.

Touch in me a stammer, Helen
Let me press you into wax, find you
again and again

I need to account for what patterns I find
to expose my daughter animal
and her movements (bare knees to bare
chest, back on wet glass),
the coming squalor

I need to bring you in,
to speak to you to bring you in

but something before me
has stained the floorboards, bodies

desert-made, skin bubbling
around earlier words

What I need is
an unquotable bloom
a heated talisman to hold

In using the world we alter the world
Don't you agree

What we see changed
by the act of seeing

I swallow here to swallow there

Quiet now on the citadel
I erase my sandal steps
the final step of burial threading
of stone slaughter

I cross my arms as evidence
and lean into the very first poem
move from pearl to shell burst
to gash of chorus

I have loved you like a mother would
drawn only what I have learned

A bitter pillowcase-feel in the mouth
a fully green leaf shaped like an antler

I don't want to live in any coming after

Any story you get now will be refusal

I knew the first of my own appetite. That to apprehend meant to look down. In the peel of the sequence I wait to hear the word *ravine* and only then put it into signs that recognize me, mark me. I don't eat at any table most of the time. I cut my mouth on a heart-spoon.

This is no argument but the violence of beacon. A shell, a staircase, other spirals, are husks but also a mode of changing and shedding, allowing for both entrance and closure. Defining and redefining the wound. I practice drawing the outline of a nautilus over the thick scar on my shoulder.

The past is self-scarring. I skin and skim myself.

And out of that shame, I am pulled into print.

I can't *listen* to the body anymore, store more of its spill. I nuzzle myself into that spiral form, a hard gold scrubbing of an image. After two hours I look up from my book to find my arm clenched and rigid at my side.

You look out from the fabric of your painting, and I into your exhausted shell.

Are you here or not-here
little film, icon
How still you become
Wreaths strung of glance
upon glance, copied
onto a bright garden floor
The form has an oily slip
a folding-over place
the sharp thread of disorder
Bodies as mine flinched
becoming larger in shadow
A girl inside the picture settles
Her hair covers up the pier-glass
She touches the body of a leaf
A signal, like when we ask
the *I* in each other

An actress friend of mine posted a picture of herself as Helen today. She has leaf eyes stab eyes, she is facing sideways. She is clean, her blood-root frozen. Little threat, little body of a leaf.

If the form of the body is the icon, I reject it. I drink this oil and I reject it.

See how I hold it in, the excess/ex-stasis, this bruise on my arm. It came to me a puddle and I lapped up its thick resin. I tell the doctor the purging is more of a *letting go*, my backchest ache yellow and bile-tight.

I don't know what I'm supposed to dial into
The nation, museum,
the institution

I stick the moon onto my bedroom wall
and look at photographs
to convince my brain of faces,
of page marks

And the woman there is heavy-collared
and plain in her sewing
Her pier-glass
thighs plodding in half-sleep

She looks up from the cover of the book
She asks me for another container
but I'm thinking of nonsense now

The old forgetting and underfeeding
Some weakless encounter
with the constant present

Knowing what I know now
I could be better
I could be a Shaker
and create things with my own gender

Mistaking wandering
for upwards

Rehearsing in advance
this disappearance

Again I wake a humming body
after dreaming of marlins

the mess of their spears
against my thigh, ocean a nagging oil
pulsing underneath

I attempt to be breathable
watch butter melt in a pan

I remember sitting in the bathtub once
seeing a child-roll, thinking
sexy, and also *how fat*

You are not benign, I thought, *not
a benign thing*,

I want to know what makes up
our bodies vs. what is being emitted
and how do we know
when to draw those lines

Driving to one place to swallow it down,
then driving to the next
to vomit it out

Becoming so undisciplined
that I can touch
and touch and all but know it

Now I am expected to sing
This story is Greek
I should be bouncing my voice
I should be between
two or three rooms, my oaken oars
half-filled with sand
I should be stiffening
with a terrible closeness
What I remember in place of
The unpictureable
I lean in to it
What is occluded here
I know grinds its lens,
holds tools in its mouth
in yet another way
to ring out this icon logic
eidolon, a hinge
crease in the hips
Yet another way to howl
in a gold shawl
To copy myself
a copy, blanketed
and justified
to pick up the telephone
with a stellar female anger,
who I am against you
against me

June. Two rings of dried pineapple and a third coffee. I write "WHAT IS THE THING?" and The Thing is always more instruction. More notes, a preparation. If we are both still alone in the gesture then there is no word one. Each ending a gap, a window.

What we know about Helen is her sex, her little form. A body of nouns. Irrepressible. She has unraveled to be yellow-haired, white-armed; the machine of Helen always was. What we know about the machine of Helen is being cited and cited and what kind of warm stone do I hold now.[2]

Every word tastes of its context. A stem, inflamed, ragged.
The part I remember. The part I don't remember. Someone
draws my blood and I blink back the gray. When I sit in a
public space my legs take up less room than his.

I believe very strongly in permanence. I keep pulling at the
stretch mark on my side. The tea olive is gold-lined and
follows me to my new house. The men are different now but
also the same, covered in crumbs, draping.

The Poet plumbs old friends. He says, *Who doesn't love to be an
instrument?* My mouth now on the book, on the symbol: an
ancestral swallow. I watch a cooking show and let my face
wander back toward the blood.

Standing with other women I wake up apart
from them, copy their length of hunger,
pleasing, expertise
Am I and what is a woman, and if I keep
repeating this question, sharing
this same body won't seem so distant
I look over and arrange and arrange and arrange
How can a body make so many mistakes

Helen, you are often overhead
when I imagine war.
The practice is always the same,
part ancient guessing, part real knowledge,
who may collapse on a chair
in this all-male house. Snow heaps
onto the book cover as a way out,
double-edged and settled on tree branches.
At night the channels open
and bombs drum on my bed through
the TV screen. In the morning
tornado sirens break in between
each dream of tornado already inside,
arching, wandering.

What I am trying to tell you
you know already—I'm olive, I'm far
orange, I am alternate shining scars
and tethers of body fat. It took me a year
to admit it, and in stillness I remember
this thicket. Inside my voice, a violet room
echoes into something more vicious.
Helen, touch the doorknob,
the house is falling. I think I should go under.

The brain shores images like a hum, a churn. All I know is to shore and accumulate, to step into these long fossils like a skirt and move from margin to margin. To write a sentence is exhausting. I hold it in. It stutters in the way that I often can. To say anything now simply hides, is not charged with hiddenness.

So I collect the routes others have taken—each decision of syntax, one word after the next. *Beloveds: We are fine and we will be fine. Beloveds: If you haven't already, evacuate immediately. Beloveds: They are unable to offer precise fire perimeter maps at this time. The fire takes us street by street.* It is only a tremble of decision, language.

Instead, the margins dissolve; words evaporate in front of me. I am at a loss for faces and look around for something not so sleek, not so un-grooved. I have carved out a studenthood to learn how to speak.

Blurred by distance, all violence is milk. Easing away from disorder renders it coherent, but all the more terrifying. Is it enough—is it enough to wave a slick flag to break the form of other?

I have nothing but dialogue here, have no other way to begin.

We could double up to hunt. We could learn to love in private, widening and Greek.

I write this breach for you, Helen. A system I've already followed before I can say *I follow*. And it is unremarkable, longing as medium. Instead of knowing, this body names. This body takes and takes its mark, the forgotten version crystal under its thumbs.

This poem you read equals the length of fission. What *I* speaks around what *I*? *I am typing this instead of writing by hand*, Adrienne Rich writes, *because my wrist on the right side / blooms and rushes with pain*.[3] Her tool of communication aches, and the answer is not *yet I am writing*, but rather *I am in pain, and therefore my writing comes to you this way*. The form becomes the telling: teeth marks on the frame.

I master open my own vessel, test out the touch. Cut my hair and pull the bloody text out from under me. Nightly now I expose the underpattern I have woven, use the pieces to make a passage. I forget other people's words, keep lists to sustain anger.

Helen, the swell in me feels the double, desires it across from me and yet it is not me. No decision my own but always against a mother, father. I fall asleep and find myself round with narrative. I am certain this museum can be summoned better by hand.

I was once beautiful in my flexibility:
the door opened, the door opened
My flatness more luminous against other
jutting skins: against hardness
I could sit and carve

A woman wears lines of a poem
in the way we find striations in our teeth
and fingernails,
bulbs of muscle tissue

Older now I address myself
by more parts to grip, how I exceed
the long bridge between
two broken pieces of poems

There is *pleasure* on the page
in sounding like a woman—

I give it up, am desert-made
no outline, no ambulance

self-containment, inviolability—
the lyric icon on the page—

The oils in my hair
radiate a dirty myth
I drink clay to heave it
onto the floor again

the Female Figure as object
which the text dominates— [4]

What else is it but a receding,
a symbol of pleading, eyes
into the ceiling,
him pushing up against

Helen, I see myself
edging bright to you

I need your lineage

your tender voltage

Who am I to be solid by
in the ravine between ancestors

I fumble toward
my coal-mining family
ask myself what mediates a distance
when a word is left rammed
and humming,
separated from its future
Each line comes achingly intact

Like a brittle fig I see you, Helen
Between the orphaned haze
of my grandmother
when I saw her sideways and alive,
in a thin picture

and later, open-
mouthed, crystalline

In class I tell my students that we must define our terms, that we must use precision in our language, or else it doesn't reach another person. In truth, one of the most telling signs that my depression is returning is that I become both bored and distrustful of poetry, of words in general. It seems so manipulative, I think, steering words around just to get other people to feel things. I am unaffected by a poet's decision to put one word in front of another word; this is just a trick.

I have seen what the flag of green language can do, am angry at my own gullibility. I find myself inside of the knowledge that language is power and that I am unpracticed in both power and its resistance. I am surviving, but in order to do so I have detached myself from the needs of the world and even of my own body, and now I am afraid I have no way to access it.

I am surviving but cannot find the shape of my own urgencies.

What is it to depend on memory but give my own so little value? To codify but delete the code? Woolf writes, *It is not a new cry, it is a very old cry.*[5]

Standing with other women I remember the tribe. I read for the silver rub of my brain about hunger and the factory. A woman wears a green shawl and calls herself *meshugganah* into the feather mattress, with words like *ravenously* and *starved*.

My mother's mother was nicknamed *Scrip* as a child because she helped distribute the scrip currency at the coal mining company where her father worked. It is etched into the inside of her high school ring that I now wear: *Scrip*. The West Virginia mining town she lived in no longer exists, has been split open and dried out. Cabin Creek District High School. I want to eat its dirt and dam.

Scrip. A name that means *token*: a note, a promise.

Once I met my sister in a room and fought to be the first body to pass through. She told me, *this is now your weight. This is now your fight.* I watch the documents now collect in me, newly-swallowed moss forming a belly. A lineage in brassy spills. In front of a mirror I measure myself in several forms, none of them manageable, none held back. *Imagine a string holding you up*, I hear. *You have two parts to your ribs; keep them buttoned together.* Here is a song in another language. I'll ask you to hold it still.

Waking too late, I feel out of symbol. I braid into others' layers. My hands fill others' pockets. Here I am slipping on the same page. Even my handwriting changes when trying to get to you.

I know I have ancestral people; the fossil record implies trial and error. I am in a café where the glass frame of a painting reflects my writing body—heavy with arms, hunting violets until barbed. Scratching into the screen I get only echoes.

Tell me what deserves intimacy, Helen. A poem is a catch-all, carries hesitation inside of it. The public orange of writing, too much, much too much. How do I decipher my own name in its largeness?

We forget words but hold each gap by the throat.

Helen, I was speaking to you when I wrote a trick about termites

I spoke to you when I wrote *the glass bends with the fecundity*
of mother termites   I spoke to the window   with my own body's
naked mirror in it   I spoke lit with sweat   with ruin
a gold peeling crust   along the ruptures   Coherence
freshly cut   What was unsaid and swallowed   turned scrim
scrimshaw   ivory yellowed from thirst   and dry heat   dry heave

This part the meat of me   the only meat of myself   the simplicity
the purge the open net   how irreducible it felt to burst hard
to destruct   to build the body then destroy it   to dread
the suspension I knew in my throat   and again   bright red
to face   my body and deflate

Form is restriction   is instruction   is no soft space   is where
I bleed above my space   I face my own carving and chain it to the floor
I trace its red wool   its calcium push and pull

How do I see it   how do I know to see   the object of a body
and how do I read   such a disappearance?

When is a throat not like a cave?

now the orange tabby outside
she wants to eat from my hand
(good women   virus   etc.)

I can hold my own form, a pulled, leadened fear
No, not form—but trunk, Helen
pained and not too separate from stellar nurseries,
from negative space/avoidant/postured/planetary/polite
too grateful to split

Open your mouth, Helen,
here is a greater
weight

it doesn't settle
it arrives
and
arrives

In this small tent men pound
on my portico, hold bees to death
in their fists. I hear their drills
slice walls, skin against nail against
bone frame of pointed organ and venom.
Against the soft holes of my body
organs press and rupture, press and rupture.
My little husk. Nothing holds upright.
I make mythical these small walls, grip a spoon
inside my mouth until the skin breaks,
here as in there. We disagree with ourselves
and choke on the institution. I run
and am stunned at how my body has created
an emergency in me. No choice now
but to go on toughening the memory, its piece
of flesh. Are we part of some heavier pattern yet?
When will men stop wasting all this energy
on transcendence? I want to write a poem where
the *I* is the one always rescuing the other *I*,
but am told over and over again that *you can't
unconsciously collaborate*. That it's just not possible.
But this is the underpattern, teeth marks
on the frame. I did not write this poem for you.
I do not write this poem.

From here the swell of growing female, allure
of being infected, it moves in and on
I feel the inertia weight, someone else's insatiability,
someone else's hunger for the sake of hunger
Yesterday you would be shrunken
and un-believed, and now your concavity
a state of matter become machine

The marble does me in again, Helen,
such heavy disregard of hair of discharge
It is far more typical to be empty,
to be made of vantage points
swollen around the icon
A beautiful corpse in a dripping towel
arms pinned underneath

To follow is to take in a liquid
Outside I am full

Being itinerant is easy, he says, The Poet says, filmed blazing and reaching across a couch. He stands for hours by brackish water, shouting the lyrical and the present, his own brassy lines in front of chemical garlands. An old mechanism to ask *how fuckable am I, how very sweetly fuckable.*

Am I a load-bearing performance, a larger and lighter watchword? Am I what whistling allegory you sang that I sang?

Nothing lives in this recording anymore, save devoted rage. Say that someone lived here, spoke here once, left this house inside-out, mastered, worked-over, and I would believe you.

I do remember language, Helen. I can't change it.
Memory is the name of this next life
and the next. There is no peace in the icon.
When I try to focus on its rosewater, its blood,
I am altogether soaked in it. I feel hunger
like a dark streak, a trick, a key word
for something left outside the room.
I dream new limps. I come to my gender
like an epithet. Somewhere else
my thighs are the ocean, a green shawl.
One thick line on my shoulder, thinner ones,
blond body hair on olive skin—spills I have
never refused. I want to call our version of things
timeless, but you tell me this is something
longer and thick with cycles.

Can I mouth this myth again and again? *Helen must remember other loves, small things. What bird, ever, was less beautiful than man?*[6]

There are 85 different kinds of pain, my physical therapist and I discuss after he gives me two broken pieces of dark Venezuelan chocolate. *The kind of pain that makes you withdraw, he says, only applies to a quarter of the 85. The rest we were born for.*

Stop tucking in your tailbone, he says.

Don't mind this language, its shriek, a fuming, less limited self. Something more than void but including the void. I fold my hands. I read *Middlemarch*. Ants fall from the ceiling and onto my bedsheets. When I roll them in my fingers they smell like dark metal. This is a symptom.

: Burrowing how you name me. Pregnant, meaning *walled-in*.
You said the skies were changeable. I felt it in the next room.

: Because Berryman said, *all has pointed HERE.*[7] Because the
baby eggplant outside already has a worm that bored its way
through. Because I don't ever feel safe.

: My nutritionist says that I am fantasizing about food too
much, will always be unsatisfied. My lungs are metallic when
I wake, this blanket a cape full of my ashes. The skyline is a
dirty haze, meals in the early hours.

: It hadn't occurred to me that I am adamant, that I am vicious. That if you aren't dead-on I'll make you dead-on. Every meal is a disappointment, this habit to swallow lost.

: I'm not looking at this leaf unless you're watching me look at this leaf. What to diffuse, to implode (this obligation). Do I know you in this language or do I *know* you?

: *How long have you been trying to lose weight?*

: Situated, not located. I'm thinking of deep pockets, muffled, some straining star. The ocean, scale-filled and buckling.

: Inscription is an act of both remembering and forgetting. Every read of this poem a healthy overturning, some sense of cycle. The center of the Milky Way as seen from the earth.

: *Did you fast before coming here?*

: *What are your feelings about boxes?*

: An animal scrapes against the metal roof and the cat goes mad.

: The tea olive outside has a hidden smell and no flowers to spot or rub up against. A family of owls and the train speak up at the same time.

: So what if I taste blood in my lungs in the cold. Over a thousand years ago a group of monks saw fire coming from the moon and it was a meteor all along.

The given of Helen is aperture.

Whatever form is is not here.

I am speaking of and for nobody now. Slash and cut. Hair parted down the middle: this is how the frame works.

I want to drop my stones to the ground, to see the grafted disorder of Helen for what it is: fragrant and good. Instead I build and build consequences, become too tired to be valuable.

In this wreckage I am a wild service. A chapter
within a chapter. I speak of hair
of leaving, messy only when I repeat myself.
Precede my own repetition.
I burrow into those
readymade cuts, let the care
carry over me. In this speaking I can take
and take my mark, but still I fall in
among animal hair and semolina.
When I scrub this old skin
it just gets older, a yellow, papered fruit
in my hands. What I read breaks
in me like a gash of atoms, the cigarette burn
on my hand a perfect, round window.

I want to know how to make a book of resisting
to make a list of foods that stayed down
when I do what I do   and I write   and waste

how very loud I waste

How loud I waste   am meat to myself too   an ornament
of doors opening and shutting   collecting fruit flies
until I wipe them away

Don't give me a subject   This memory is ruin   is ruin
The subject of this memory   is ruin

I have had years of cleanliness
have carved a candle out of starving

Now I want any warm thing

What to calibrate now, am I
conflicted, this backhanded pain
in my chest, someone's dark belief
of a body. I mean to speak of primacy,
to mark by incision but am at a loss,
a flag shaking toward the cold
and the good. Riots end
and don't end. Any loss knows
this: though small against it
the winds still come. The speaking
subject is continual disappointment.
I've defined it. This museum
its artifice, war thrashing at its lens.
All I wanted was to make contact
and still I tell only stories of an echo.
Is it better to have misgivings
than to imagine a woman without face
or hands, and is this even a new cry?

We find rupture in those first sentences
Glaciers, a thawing space of power and hard fabric
Don't tell me about the wreck of forgetting
I refuse to answer the question as asked,
stagger out to punch an ode into the cosmos
An unending child, waiting to be shook open
I   the day cracks   I am that child

My comrades and I, we continue
our bloody mary lunch in the Rainier fog,
make peace with a toxic sex, a real
hanging fear
that we are never safe

That pulling my tights up is a sign. That leaning over to pull up my tights is a sign. That the man over there is stopping and touching himself and that is my fault and my tights' fault.

That I will never know what my body is doing and I will hear always someone tell me to put it away, to discipline it, a body, another body, my body.

Under hold of this threat: little girl waiting to be shook open around a nice man who will inevitably do bad things. That everywhere she goes, there will be a nice man who will do bad things.

I write to convince my comrades that our bodies (always abstract, always slipping from under us) are heavy thrones, much stronger than they are weak. Shark skin and Velcro, running thighs, glass bodice. How difficult it is to keep up.

Before I was born I had a name but no gender. I was confused with a water parasite. When I was born the doctor told my mother, *she's too pretty to be anything but a girl.*

The very nature of memory is violent. Barthes writes of the punctum, the puncture; in his *Mourning Diary* he is constantly *lacerated* by surprise presences and absences. *Struck by the abstract nature of absences,* he says, *yet it's so painful, lacerating. Which allows me to understand abstraction somewhat better: it is absence and pain, the pain of absence—perhaps therefore love?).*[8] But only violent enough to engrave, not to alter time itself—that is trauma's domain.

I know that when a man went to prison I was six years old, not entirely unaware. I cried and was afraid the ballerina platypus toy he gave me had cameras in its plush. In the bathtub my hand would brush against my chest and a slurry of nausea would follow.

Woolf: *I could not pass it / dumb horror.*[9]

I say *I'm working on a poem thinking about.*

I say *this is a poem vector. This is a vector towards.*

I say *I'm working on a feminist serial poem. Towards anger, towards trauma.*

I say *I have nothing to give, and it tastes sour.*

I say *I wake with a mouth full of chicory, of woodworm.*

I say *there are no other words for what I mean by body.*

I say *I'd recommend not reading it at all, but it's what I've been marinating on if I'm not writing Helen poems and then this just sort of came out.*

I say *And one part is something I've been meaning to say, that it just sort of came to me a few weeks ago, and*

I say *it's not a poem, but maybe after doing this I can figure out what else to write about, it's been bothering me in these kinds of poems.*

I say *This is not a poem.*

I say *Whatever, it's Easter, the day of being renewed, right?*

This is not a poem. I have no language,
gesture loudly around the gallery
in the shape of something like shame.
Each word a covering-up of something
I haven't done. Each ending a calling out,
a final, watery note to be repeated
without resolution. A feral litany
of what is left. An aluminum carcass
I hold in my teeth. There is no middle
ground of taking back. Tread appears
no matter the move.

When I was born I was born good.

"Did they re-touch her arms, her shoulders?
did anyone touch her ever?"[10]

– *Helen in Egypt*, H.D.

How did she hold a nectarine? Who stood, kissing
her belly like the ship's bow? What did she see in silk
stockings, in the breasted light of the gray pier-glass?
Were her eyes screened and away? Was her dress
blue-dashed and signal-heavy? Did her hard, oaken scars
show through? Did she at all find me here, painted
with the telephone of her? Was she more afraid of fog
or a field, living room or bank? How did she move
through this caroled multiverse? Had she seen a glacier,
filled with rivets and the bodies of mermaids?
What glowing berries did she hold in her lap, waiting
for the snow to start? Was she always told when
to be full, when not to be? Did she write *the fecundity*
of mother termites when she wanted to write *eating disorder*?
Was she glad to have me in her future? Did she hear
the daughter upstairs watching *National Velvet*?
How often did she speak of willing bodies to be good?
Did she alone have a throbbing lightness, a courage
in defining some quick green beginning? How, then,
did she recover the hyacinth body, my body, like her body?

Helen has no idea we are here. My comrades, my beautiful comrades. We watch the veil of milk leave a woman's face, her breasts bare. The raw parts of her skin are salamander pink until gray. Don't wash her face, her cheeks, her ruddy jaw. I will say *woman* to talk about someone else. I am a girl starfish, gutted clean.

(I once wrote a poem for a friend, and it ended *I am still alive she said / hand me the wooden spoon.*

The next year she died and I thought it was on a mountain but it was at home in her bed. She had a canary tattooed on her thigh, so that perhaps she might get up off of the roof/out of her vomit; instead she flickered out.)

Helen, this is for you and it is unremarkable. Some part of a solar eclipse ends before it begins. I used to think that I could only know memory through what came out of me. A grain taste. Pressing out to mark what's inside. The base of my throat, an object: bulb and water.

We try to make memories pieces of flesh, threads of leather we grab and mouth.

I've forgotten most of this already, even though I just typed it out.

This, and this. This, and this.

When is a throat not like a cave? My question is about being stalled, about intimacy. I am learning what it means to swallow this gold thread, to let the scatter keep itself in me, scatter over me for years.

You offer a blankness, Helen, and I am learning how to speak to you. How very loud I carve into the old voices. When I yawn, my littered body opens out like a cup for you.

I am surprised at how long it took for me to be angry. Or to know I have always been angry. To outline this anger into the form into the pier-glass.

No one is here to see me pick up this leaf,
swaying in the dirt of my own female
Knowing well the rearranging
and how we neglect the vault
Nature continues to be a hidden talk,
slipping at its labels
and all I remember is the maddening host
we continue to allow in our evening bodies,
rearranging ice to swaddle the nodes
Calibrations in my throat
to not freeze out

You can heat my body, Helen
but it will only make the virus grow faster

I want to talk about hubris. The carpeted atria of hubris.

To think I could carry women on my back.

To think that I could track self and other was hubris.

My comrades, my beautiful comrades—they know the tiny creature of Helen, they know who I talk to. That I am superstitious to put things into writing. That I don't trust hypotheticals. They know the powder I make in this language.

I want a way to talk about my body without calling it a body, a female body. I want to see something—

I am looking for scale here.

I want to name, to articulate, to hold THE THING, the loss.

But I cannot touch Helen—Helen of Troy, my aunt Helen, mothers a mother again and again. I don't want to touch her. This is hubris. A loop of a phantom who thought she was underwater, who did not document, and I cannot write what she needs.

Where is her golden armpit? Where is linearity? Who is responsible?

What warm stone do I hold now?

In the weeks before I moved, I watched videos of Inuit throat singing while packing boxes. I watched a mother and a daughter in a blue-white kitchen, I saw her and I saw her, and they were facing each other to be a part of the other's body, beating their hoof sounds against the other's throat.

When I sing I feel like I cannot be human, says my favorite singer.[11]

At first I think they sound hardened, bone-angry, but this isn't true. These are growls from a slow, slow land, past and outside of anger. They are *ecstatic*, a word formed of the prefix *ek* (outside or beyond) and *stasis* (standing, position). Outside position. A radical discontinuity. They are at a stand-off with language.

A sound below singing, this is a call and response of feral breathing, of women. The low lows never leave the box of the body. Both inhale and exhale are a calling out. Moon-throated, they face the other, hold her by the arms. I watch them as they bear down into, as they touch, the underpattern.

Each singer leaves gaps for the other to fill in, vertices. The most intimate spaces, vertices can either be convex or concave. Spaces open for tenderness, like the inside of a knee.

You want to sing like a zipper, one daughter says, each tooth pulling into the other's space.

Compassion is in the zippered teeth, the inhale to exhale.

I live in Michigan now; men still work on the house next door. I wave at them every morning when I take my puppy out to pee. The puppy blinks in the sun and turns into water. His skin is black and gold until he stretches it white.

On the other side of my house are five men in a Christian brotherhood who have committed to communal living. On this side, I pinch my thigh to come back. I come back, sit hard. Sit through the very same motions of purge and battle, olive and caul. Some wide-eyed throat opens, goes on opening. Through the silence where I find myself being born, where I have left my own disaster in a hollowed out tree as a nest.

What I am trying to say is: this book is a process of learning to speak again, of continuing to practice the problem. Of leaning into devotion when it is bleak.

It was either Helen or the present tense of absence, which is bigger, browner than the language it comes in. An upward itch, the flicker of the breach. It was a way of saying *sometimes you're nothing but meat*, the meat of me at all. A calibration of what the me body is vs. the you body vs. the wave body: rigor, root-tangled. The wave body, ravenous for seawater, humming in its refusal—of coherence, of mutilation. The wave body out of the frame, looking back in through the violets.

I write Helen as a wave body.

From here a skein, a solution:
harbinger of an opening

A little note from beyond, i.e.,
the lost family joke, the long bridge
between moments of being
and their reverb

Should I not be supremely content
that a fire is built instead of made,
made instead of male

That in the pockets of this overcoat
I am female, a form of being bold but not bold

red in eyelet, repeating *I am 27, I am 27*
to too many doctors
and the tea olive's hidden smell

a sense of stalemate overhead

an obligation to make angles and lose
this animal body
to sing about and value preparedness
like something we weave and erect a fort under

To deserve this realm of history
in no language

Never mind the shriek on the radio:

A hemorrhage subsiding
a long file of rain

Dear Helen, our dead
names are on your tongue
each gape a wound
of gold thread, patient
as the teardrop shape
of a hand as it dances
through the other hand
I wait until the hunger returns,
ever small this loss of canopy
That it is difficult to settle
this hollow, that I bleed above
my lip and don't mind
the mechanism: that I deserve
this riddled hunger

[1] H.D., *Helen in Egypt* (New York: New Directions, 1974), 1.

[2] Homer describes Helen in the *Iliad* as "white-armed," "long-robed," and "richly-tressed," leaving the rest up to imagination. "White-armed" connotes class, purity, and divinity more than race. Post-antiquity representations, however, tend to show a whiter Helen, with reddish or blonde hair (see pre-Raphaelite paintings). H.D.'s "Helen," written many years before *Helen in Egypt*, depicts a "wan and white" Helen—almost a statue—with "still eyes in the white face" that "all Greece hates" (*Collected Poems 1912–1944*, 154–155). Her hair has been described as "ξανθὸς" which is often translated to "blonde"—although this too is up for some debate. Anne Carson's translation of Sappho "Fragment 23" reveals "]and to yellowhaired Helen I liken you" (Sappho, trans. Anne Carson, *If not, winter: Fragments of Sappho*, 43).

[3] Adrienne Rich, "Contradictions: Tracking Poems" in *Later Poems: Selected and New 1971–2012* (New York: Norton, 2013), 164–179.

[4] Rachel Blau DuPlessis, "Otherhow," in *The Pink Guitar: Writing as Feminist Practice* (New York: Routledge, 1990), 142.

[5] "As we listen to the voices we seem to hear an infant crying in the night, the black night that now covers Europe, and with no language but a cry, Ay, ay, ay, ay . . . But it is not a new cry, it is a very old cry. Let us shut off the wireless and listen to the past.": Virginia Woolf, *Three Guineas* (New York: Harvest, 1963), 128–9.

[6] H.D., *Helen in Egypt* (New York: New Directions, 1974), 165.

[7] John Berryman, *Recovery* (New York: Farrar, Straus, and Giroux, 1973), 73.

[8] Roland Barthes, *Mourning Diary* (New York: Farrar, Straus, and Giroux, 2010), 42.

[9] Virginia Woolf, *Moments of Being* (New York: Harvest, 1985), 71, 78.

[10] H.D., *Helen in Egypt* (New York: New Directions, 1974), 245.

[11] "Episode 7: Arctic Crossroads" in *The Polar Sea* (Primitive Entertainment, 2014). Singer is vocalist Tanya Tagaq.

ACKNOWLEDGMENTS

I am grateful to the editors of the following publications in which poems from this book first appear, sometimes in earlier forms: *Bennington Review*, *B O D Y*, *Bone Bouquet*, *Dusie*, *elsewhere*, *Entropy*, *Ghost Proposal*, *Gulf Coast*, *interrupture*, *jubilat*, *MiPOesias*, *Muse A/Journal*, *New South Journal*, *NightBlock*, *Powder Keg*, *Smoking Glue Gun*, *TIMBER*, *TYPO*, *The Volta: They Will Sew the Blue Sail*, and *The Wanderer*. An essay written out of this process was published in *American Poetry Review* ("Reading Ekstasis: Tracking Contradictions, Sustaining Incongruences").

Thank you to Caroline Cabrera and Anne Cecelia Holmes for being my constant go-tos in all matters Helen-related. They read these poems as embryos and remain my main sources of critique, dialogue, and support.

Thank you to my dissertation committee members at UGA—Ed Pavlic, Magdalena Zurawski, and Andrew Zawacki—for their patience, rigor and friendship. Thank you to Susan Rosenbaum, whose critical insights— implicit or explicit—are throughout this book. I am ever grateful to Dara Wier for her guidance, comfort, and dinners many years ago, for a strange and delightful study in risk and chance, and for giving me some first kernels of hope that I could sustain my own book-length endeavor.

Endless gratitude to friends and colleagues who over the years acted as generous readers, corresponders, sources of inspiration, providers of meals, and without whom this project would not exist. Special thanks to Lindsay Tigue, Alex Edwards, Colette Arrand, Caroline Crew, Dennis James Sweeney, Oliver Baez Bendorf and Kim Charles Kay, Jenny Krichevsky, Ryan Collins, Jake Syersak, and Shamala Gallagher. Carrie Lorig: for the rigor and brilliance of your work, correspondence, and friendship, I am indebted to you.

Thank you to my students and colleagues in Amherst, Athens, Grand Rapids, and Young Harris.

Gratitude to the Vermont Studio Center, Kimmel Harding Nelson Center for the Arts, and the Willson Center for Humanities and Art at UGA for their support to finish this book. Thank you to the Beinecke Rare Book and Manuscript Library at Yale University for access to the H.D. Papers and Archive.

Endless gratitude to the team at YesYes Books, and to the insightful editing of KMA Sullivan.

Thank you to my family: near, far, and growing ever-bigger. Thank you to my mother for giving me her name. This book began the month my grandmother—Scrip—died. Her Farness is more Near.

p. 7 ["To name her is desire"]
This piece is in deep gratitude to Dennis James Sweeney.

p. 8 ["With lemon voices they called you"]:
This piece borrows phrasing from David Farrell Krell, *Of Memory, Reminiscence, and Writing: On the Verge* (Bloomington: Indiana UP, 1990), 15. (" . . . and only those creatures that have a sense of time—that is, of passage, lapse, rupture, or ekstasis, as an ek tinos eis ti—can be said to remember.").

p. 26 ["Every word tastes of its context"]:
This piece borrows phrasing from M.M. Bakhtin, "Discourse in the Novel," *The Dialogic Imagination*, ed. by Michael Holquist, trans. Caryl Emerson and Michael Holquist (Austin: University of Texas Press, 1981), 293.

p. 29 ["The brain shores images"]:
"Charged with hiddenness" is in dialogue with *The H.D. Book* by Robert Duncan, eds. Michael Boughn and Victor Coleman (Berkeley: U of California Press, 2011), 7.

p. 35 ["Standing with other women I remember the tribe"]:
This piece refers to two short stories by Anzia Yezierska: "Wings," and "Hunger," from *Hungry Hearts* (New York: Penguin Books, 1997).

p. 37 ["Helen, I was speaking to you"]:
This piece (and p. 63 ["When is a throat not like a cave?"]) is in dialogue with "What is the human throat if not a cave?": Bruce Bond, *Immanent Distance: Poetry and the Metaphysics of the Near at Hand* (Ann Arbor: University of Michigan Press), 177.

p. 67 ["I live in Michigan now"]:
This piece began as an assignment from *Ghost Proposal* (ghostproposal.com) and borrows phrases from Phoebe Glick's work in Issue 7, as well as "Blood Roses" by Tori Amos; the phrase "Coherence is mutilation" is from "The Departure of the Train" by Clarice Lispector.

GALE MARIE THOMPSON is the author of *Helen Or My Hunger* (YesYes Books, 2020), *Soldier On* (Tupelo Press, 2015), and two chapbooks, including *Expeditions to the Polar Seas* (Sixth Finch, 2013). Raised in Georgia and South Carolina, Gale received a B.A. from the College of Charleston, an M.F.A. in Poetry from the University of Massachusetts Amherst, and a Ph.D. in English Literature and Creative Writing from the University of Georgia. Her work has appeared in *Crazyhorse, American Poetry Review, BOAAT, Gulf Coast, Tin House Online, Guernica, jubilat*, and *Bennington Review*, among others. She has received fellowships from the Vermont Studio Center and Kimmel Harding Nelson Center for the Arts and has given workshops and craft talks for the Emily Dickinson Museum, O, Miami Foundation, Midwest Writing Center, and others. Gale is the founding editor of *Jellyfish Poetry* and has worked on the editorial teams of *jubilat, Crazyhorse, Fairy Tale Review, Georgia Review*, and Slope Editions. She lives in the mountains of North Georgia, where she directs the creative writing program at Young Harris College.

ALSO FROM YESYES BOOKS

FICTION
Girls Like Me by Nina Packebush

RECENT FULL-LENGTH COLLECTIONS
Ugly Music by Diannely Antigua
To Know Crush by Jennifer Jackson Berry
Gutter by Lauren Brazeal
What Runs Over by Kayleb Rae Candrilli
This, Sisyphus by Brandon Courtney
Salt Body Shimmer by Aricka Foreman
Forever War by Kate Gaskin
Ceremony of Sand by Rodney Gomez
Undoll by Tanya Grae
Everything Breaking / For Good by Matt Hart
Sons of Achilles by Nabila Lovelace
Landscape with Sex and Violence by Lynn Melnick
GOOD MORNING AMERICA I AM HUNGRY AND ON FIRE by jamie mortara
Stay by Tanya Olson
a falling knife has no handle by Emily O'Neill
One God at a Time by Meghan Privitello
I'm So Fine: A List of Famous Men & What I Had On by Khadijah Queen
If the Future Is a Fetish by Sarah Sgro
Gilt by Raena Shirali
Boat Burned by Kelly Grace Thomas

RECENT CHAPBOOK COLLECTIONS

Vinyl 45s

Inside My Electric City by Caylin Capra-Thomas

Exit Pastoral by Aidan Forster

Of Darkness and Tumbling by Mónica Gomery

The Porch (As Sanctuary) by Jae Nichelle

Juned by Jenn Marie Nunes

Unmonstrous by John Allen Taylor

Preparing the Body by Norma Liliana Valdez

Giantess by Emily Vizzo

Blue Note Editions

Beastgirl & Other Origin Myths by Elizabeth Acevedo

Kissing Caskets by Mahogany L. Browne

One Above One Below: Positions & Lamentations by Gala Mukomolova

Companion Series

Inadequate Grave by Brandon Courtney

The Rest of the Body by Jay Deshpande